With Love...

With

Love...

by ROD McKUEN

STANYAN BOOKS

RANDOM HOUSE

For Mary

CONTENTS

With Love...

SCHOOL

Before the Palmer method
taught me how
to write my name,
I'd learned to read <u>love</u>
in the salesman's face.

And so
without the aid of Dick and Jane,
by myself I've come
unadorned and plain
to offer you without condition
a life just past
and just beginning.

WOOD SMOKE

The geese above the pond
already call out winter
and wood smoke comes
from all the houses
in the town.

We'll move together then
and share the year's last
        warmness
swallowing the rain like brandy.

ATLAS

Don't be afraid
to fall asleep with gypsies
            or run with leopards.
As travelers or highwaymen
we should employ
whatever kind of wheels it takes
to make our lives
            go smoothly down the road.

And if you love somebody
            tell them.
Love's a better roadmap
for trucking down the years
than Rand McNally ever made.

DECLARATION

Your mouth
is my undoing.
So it is and so it should be.

Closed or open,
private or in public places
I covet your mouth,
often hearing not a word
that issues from it
but knowing every sound
            by heart.

Love, I do
and it's a new release
I should have come upon
a dozen years ago.
I did.
It's only that you didn't know.

TO PAUSE

I've run the corridors
and highways of the heart
for so long now
I find it difficult to pause,
let alone to stop.

But a pause is just
another kind of stop.

I glance both ways though,
(I wouldn't take a chance
on missing love
wherever she may lurk.)

BOXING LESSONS

Wiser by a half a year
I enter into your brown body
like a blind man sure of every step.
So assured
               sometimes I feel embarrassed.

So delighted that I wonder
how I earned the privilege
of your light limbs around my back.

If indeed I've earned
your body and your love
then I'll return
               undefeated.
A lover who by accident
               or even by design

stumbled into something
so unusual yet real
he comes back blushing
from every new encounter
with your touch.

THE PRIZE

After each new meeting with you
I carry home
so much love
that I must have set
a brand new mark in selfishness.

I've won all the races,
all the prizes never offered.

If I tell you this
and make it work for me
I might be beautiful enough
to even have your love.

TOWARD SECURITY

June is for juggling
getting rid of spring
and moving into summertime.
The beach is but a back rest waiting
                to fold down into August.

In love,
we walk a tight-rope
as new brides dash
from Cincinnati churches
and rejects sling their rings
                into the Reno river.

When the sand starts singing
nobody else will hear but us.

THE DISTANCE TO MONTEREY

Silence is a better means
for telegraphing thought
than any Morse code yet made.
I wonder if you know
how many conversations
we've had so far
with no words passed?
I often think our silence
has energy to get us
all the way to Monterey and back.

THE MEANING OF GIFTS

Before befriending butterflies
you have to meet with midnight moths.
Perspective comes when poles
are far enough apart
              to have horizons at both ends.

So trampling through the night together
lying close with moonlight faces
              will never be enough.
We'll have to beat each other down
              by daylight
to understand why love is love
and why it's come to us in March
              three months ahead of summer.

IN PASSING

Yesterday,
did you remember how we met?

Today,
do you remember what I said?

Tomorrow,
will you remember how I tasted?
Some have said I taste like almonds.

TEARING DOWN WALLS

No wall can stop the coming of love
no clock can bring it back,

yet letters are still sent on missions
armies couldn't win, for love or country.

RUNNER

I have no time to hate,
I'm in a hurry.

But I've got all the hours
in the days still left to me
to waste on love.

And what a waste
of God's free time
to not love readily
                and straight ahead.

FOOTPRINTS

Not content to fly to Cedar Falls
I'd like to track the footprints on the moon
and come back home with bouquets of spare junk.
Since there's so little mystery left
        in moonlight through the window
I'd like to bring you one handful
to decorate your dressing table.

Women want the near impossible.
Knowing that,
the wise man stays ready.

We ask the difficult ourselves.
        Love us.
    For ourselves.

WE THOUGHT PERHAPS

We know the clocks are changing
                    but we've come prepared.
The three of us have run all day
and all the season too.

You might expect us to be tired.
                    No.

It's just that after thumbing
                    beach to beach
we thought perhaps
that somewhere in our travels
                    going from the sand
                        or coming from the water
we might have accidentally come by you.

A loss.
But totaling this summer's gains
would not be fair.
And anyway how do you write down secrets
and make them not so secret any more?

The three of us
(the dogs and me)
are maybe tired after all.

But we still hope to see you
one more time
coming down the beach.

APPLES

If you like apples
I'll carry home an orchard.
If sky is to your liking
I'll bundle up the skies
              of summer
so you'll never need to know
the winter evening any more.

I like the fire
and so I wait for winter nights.
Apples I can take or leave.

Your body
like your mind
has need of going over,
and I intend to be
a journeyman of your soft skin
                        for years.

LATE OCTOBER

Always, then,
and ever afterward
the head against
        the shoulder
when the thunder comes.

It will be so
as night is for the nightingales
so love will last for me.

Welcome is the thunder,
if you go or stay.

FURROWS

Often I feel
the furrows on your forehead
are deep enough
to make a proper trench—
        and then you grin.

DID YOU KNOW?

The air was bearable to me
only just because I had to breathe
but then you must have known that.

I don't think
I could have stood
the green of green trees
too much longer on my own
—even though I had no way
of knowing what I'd missed
by not sharing
          until you stood my bail
              by being here.

KEEPING WITH TRADITION

If I can walk with April people
                    all year long
I ought to do as well in April.

So as one whose Aprils have been many
I'll hunt for lilacs once again
and hope that spring's
as good to me this year as last.
Without those friends
I've found the fourth month in
I haven't any friends at all.

With Katie gone
and Kelly growing more sophisticated
          day by day
my life should have some lilacs
at the very least.

April then and always when?

CYCLE

Only lonely men know freedom.
Love,
as lovely as it is,
still ensnares.

Is it better then
to be on the outside,
in the dark and free,
or caged contentedly
but still looking
out beyond the bars.

OLD HOUSES

I love old houses
          for their smells,
their must and dust and mildew
and for what they've been
to people I will never know.

The character
of calked-up cracks
means more to me
than plastered walls and pretty paper,
walls that play the neighbors' music
when the radio I love
          has gone to sleep.

The faces of the old
are like old houses
every line's a highway
                    from the past.

And so I love old houses
and the faces that sit rocking
on their sagging porches.

THE ADVENTURES OF CLARK KENT

Your body lying easy in the August day
is not a challenge but an invitation.
Being lazy too
        I leave it to the sun to ravage.

Night—always more dependable than sunshine
has a way of coming 'round on time
and I'm a patient man.

Don't think I haven't noticed
those intrepid hikers of the summer beach
who in the guise of Sunshine Supermen
live out the tail ends of the afternoons
behind half Venetian blinds
with what they've staked out on mid-mornings.

Notice though
the rope I've tied about your ankle.
No Latin sun can steal my mistress
for more than just one single afternoon.

CLOSE

Forward or back
September is the turning time.
Ask the man whose livelihood is apples
or the man who lives for love.

So spreading our arms wide
we gather in September,
as a cold man searching after firewood
before the snow blots out the world.

WATER MUSIC

There are rivers
that I'll never see.
That never worried me
                        till now.

But as a soldier of the heart
I've this year
        come to fear,
that on some battlefield
not yet near,
upon the final stream
                        I'll fall.

With that in mind
I ford each river
as I would the last
and take each lover
as I would
       that final
           fatal one.

TELL ME HOW THE WIND BLOWS

Tell me how the wind blows,
and what it takes to find
new waves rolling
down new beaches
and different drummers
          drumming somewhere—
              if they do.

Tell me lies,
and if your honesty's a badge
then wear it out of sight.

Especially if you intend
to disavow your love for me.

WITH LOVE...

I do what I do with love.
Criticize you might.
But I'll match you sleep for sleep
      night for night.

ABOUT THE AUTHOR

ROD McKUEN was born in Oakland, California, in 1933, and grew up in California, Nevada, Washington and Oregon. He has traveled extensively, both as a concert artist and as a writer. In the past three years his books of poetry have sold in excess of three million copies in hardcover, making him the best-selling poet not only of this age but probably of every other era as well. In addition, he is the composer of more than a thousand popular songs and several film scores, including The Prime of Miss Jean Brodie (for which his song received an Academy Award nomination). Artists such as Frank Sinatra, Petula Clark, Glenn Yarbrough, Rock Hudson, Claudette Colbert and Don Costa have devoted entire albums to his compositions.

His major classical works, Symphony #1, Concerto for 4 Harpsichords and Orchestra and Concerto for Guitar and Orchestra, have been performed by leading American symphony orchestras as well as those in foreign capitals of the world.

Before becoming a best-selling author and composer, Mr. McKuen worked as a laborer, radio disc jockey and newspaper columnist, and as a psychological-warfare scriptwriter during the Korean War.

He is currently writing screenplays based on his first two books of poetry and is about to make his debut as a film director.

When not traveling, he lives at home in California in a rambling Spanish house with a menagerie of sheepdogs, cats and a turtle named Wade.